The Railway Rabbits

Bracken and the Wild Bunch

Georgie Adams

Illustrated by Anna Currey

Orion
Children's Books

First published in Great Britain in 2012
by Orion Children's Books
a division of the Orion Publishing Group Ltd
Orion House
5 Upper St Martin's Lane
London WC2H 9EA
An Hachette UK Company

1 3 5 7 9 10 8 6 4 2

The Orion Publishing Group's policy is to use papers that are
natural, renewable and recyclable products and made from wood
grown in sustainable forests. The logging and manufacturing
processes are expected to conform to the environmental regulations
of the country of origin.

A catalogue record for this book is available from the British Library.

Printed in Great Britain by Clays Ltd, St. Ives plc.

ISBN 978 1 4440 0257 7

www.orionbooks.co.uk
www.georgieadams.com

The
Railway
Rabbits

Bracken and the Wild Bunch

Look out for more adventures with
The Railway Rabbits . . .

For wildlife everywhere –

G.A.

The Ripple River Valley

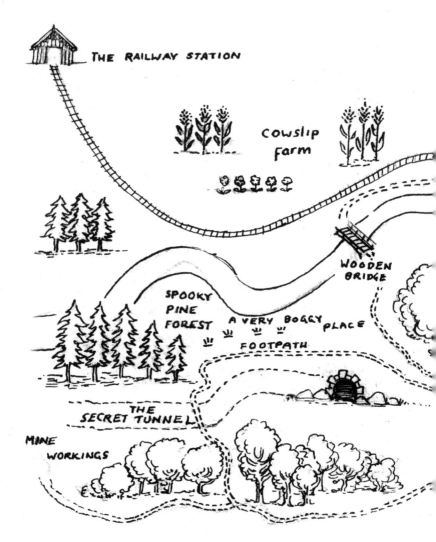

THE RAILWAY STATION

COWSLIP FARM

WOODEN BRIDGE

SPOOKY PINE FOREST

A VERY BOGGY PLACE

FOOTPATH

THE SECRET TUNNEL

MINE WORKINGS

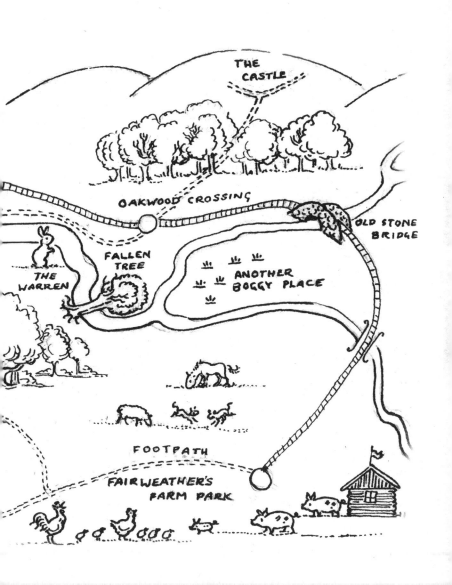

THE CASTLE

OAKWOOD CROSSING

OLD STONE BRIDGE

THE WARREN

FALLEN TREE

ANOTHER BOGGY PLACE

FOOTPATH

FAIRWEATHER'S FARM PARK

Bracken
Runs
Away
1

One night, Bracken Longears woke with
a start. He could hear a low whistling
noise and wondered what it was. There it
was again! This time the noise was much
nearer. Bracken jumped up, bumped
his head on the burrow roof and trod on
Bramble – all at the same time.

"Ouch!" said Bramble. "Mind my tail."

"Ow!" said Bracken, rubbing his
gingery-brown head.

The rabbits woke their parents,
Barley and Mellow, who came to see
what was the matter. "What's going on?"
said Barley.

"It's the middle of the night,"
said Mellow.

"I heard a noise," said Bracken.

Berry, Fern and Wisher rushed from
their sleeping hollows to join them. Fern
looked worried.

"What s-s-sort of a noise, Bracken?" she said. "Was it a rat? A f-f-fox? What was it?"

"It was more like a whistle," Bracken said.

"Maybe you heard a mouse?" said Berry.

"Or the wind?" said Wisher.

The rabbits huddled together and listened.

After a few minutes, Bramble broke the silence.

"Huh! I can't hear anything," he said.

"Bracken woke us up for nothing!"

"You scared me," said Fern.

"Sorry," said Bracken. He felt a bit silly, but he was sure he'd heard something.

"Never mind," said Mellow. "Let's all go back to bed."

Next morning, Barley, Mellow and the five young rabbits hurried up-burrow to look for something to eat. It had been raining in the night and the grass felt wet beneath their paws. Berry jumped over a molehill and landed in a puddle – SPLASH!

"Ugh!" said Berry, water dripping from his ears.

"Trust you to do something silly," said Mellow, smiling.

Just then, Bracken spotted a clump of yellow flowers on tall stalks growing in the meadow.

"Cowslips! Yummy!" he said. Cowslips are a rabbit's favourite food.

Bracken ran over to them and started eating.

The others were quick to follow. In his hurry to get to the plants, Bramble pushed Bracken out of the way.

"Hey!" said Bracken. "That's not fair." I saw them first."

"So what?" said Bramble, his mouth
full. "It wasn't fair you trod on my tail
last night."

"And made up a silly noise,"
said Berry.

"And woke us up," said Fern. "It took
me ages to go back to sleep."

"I was a bit scared," said Wisher.

"I did hear a noise!" said Bracken.
"Why is everybody picking on me?"

But no one was listening. They were
far too busy eating cowslips. Nobody
noticed Bracken slip away and go

towards the river. He felt unhappy and
unwanted. He sat by the wooden bridge
to think.

"I know I heard something last night,"
he said. "And I saw those cowslips before
anyone else. Slugs and snails! It isn't fair!"

"What isn't?" said a familiar voice.

Bracken turned.

Sylvia Squirrel was sitting by a small
heap of acorns. Bracken told her what
had happened.

"Well," said Sylvia. "You were right
about the whistling. I heard it too."

"You did?" said Bracken.

"Yes," said Sylvia. "I don't know what or who was making it. Mind you, a few new creatures have come to live here, ever since people-folk made the woods and riverbank a better place for animals. I spotted a lizard sunning itself on the bridge earlier today."

Bracken nodded. He remembered a time not so long ago when his family and friends had been worried that people-folk were going to destroy their homes. But to everyone's relief, they'd discovered people-folk were trying to help them.

"I saw a grass snake the other day," he told Sylvia. "Marr told me what it was. Maybe they whistle at night?"

"Maybe," said Sylvia. "Anyway, I can't stop any longer. I must find a place to hide my acorns."

With a twitch of her tail, Sylvia ran behind the tree trunk and was gone.

Alone again, Bracken wondered what he should do. If I go home and tell the others that Sylvia Squirrel heard the whistling noise too, will anyone believe me? Bramble will probably say I'm telling stories! Bracken was a little afraid of his brother and didn't want to argue with him. But it wasn't just Bramble. Bracken was cross with the rest of his family for not believing him about the whistling noise.

"Hm!" he said. "Everyone always believes Wisher when she says her ears are tingling and she can hear voices. So why won't they listen to me?"

After thinking for a while longer, Bracken had an idea. A BIG idea.

"I'll run away!" he said. "I won't go far. I don't want to stay out all night. Not with foxes and whistling snakes about. Bramble, Berry, Fern and Wisher will soon realise I'm missing. Marr will worry her whiskers off. Parr might send out a search party! And then everyone will be pleased when I come home, and Bramble will be sorry he was mean to me."

Bracken felt much better. It was a good plan and he'd thought of it all by himself. He looked up and down the riverbank and decided to take the path to the left of the wooden bridge.

It was then he saw the paw prints.

Along the Paw Print Path
2

Bracken stared at the tracks. "I wonder who made these?" he said.

He took a closer look. The paw prints stood out clearly on the muddy path. The pad was almost round. Each print showed five toes spread apart with five claw pricks.

He was a bit worried. From the size
of the paw prints, Bracken thought they
must belong to quite a large animal.

Parr would know what they are, he
thought. Barley had taught all the young
rabbits how to recognise the tracks of
some animals – especially their enemies.
Bracken knew, for example, that these
prints were larger than a dog's, or a
fox's. Bracken's heart beat faster and
for a split-second he thought about
running back to his burrow. Then he
shook his head.

"I don't want Bramble to think I'm a scaredy-rabbit," he said. "Sylvia Squirrel says she's seen a few new animals on the riverbank or maybe these tracks belong to one of them. Or maybe they belong to the animal who made that whistling noise last night. I'll find out what it is and tell everyone. Then they'll have to believe me. Marr and Parr will be proud of me. Bramble will think I'm very clever!"

Bracken set off along the path, following the trail of paw prints. The mid-morning sun warmed his back. The muddy tracks were soon dry in the heat. He hadn't gone far when a sudden movement caught his eye.

It was Violet Vole. She was busy
clearing roots and stones from
her tunnel in the riverbank.
Violet stopped what she
was doing when she
saw him.

"Hello," she said. "Out
and about on your own today?"

"Yes," said Bracken. "I'm following
these paw prints. Do you know who they
belong to?"

"Well," said Violet. "Yes and no."

Bracken was puzzled.

"Which?" he said.

"Both," said Violet. "Yes, I did see who
made them. No, I don't know who it was.
A strange, wild-looking creature . . ."

"What was it like?" said Bracken
excitedly.

"I couldn't see very well," said Violet.

"It was last night. Something woke me up. A sort of whistling noise. I popped my head out to see what it was, but the moon slipped behind a cloud and it started to rain and . . ."

"Please, Violet," said Bracken. "What did you see?"

"I was just about to say," said Violet. "Where was I? Ah, yes. It had a long body and short legs. I think it had a tail. Yes. A thick tail."

"Anything else?" said Bracken.

"Not that I can remember," said Violet. "Now, I must get on. I'm spring cleaning. Goodbye!"

Violet disappeared down a hole and Bracken continued on his way. Soon afterwards, he met another friend. Hazel Heron was standing on one leg by the edge of the river.

"Hello," said Hazel. "All on your own today, Bracken? Where are the others?"

"At home," said Bracken. Then, before Hazel could ask any more questions: "I'm on the trail of a strange animal. Have you seen one?"

"Yes, I have!" said Hazel. "It was earlier this morning. The cheeky creature stole a fish from right under my beak!"

"Wow!" said Bracken.

"It came from the path," said Hazel. "I'd just spotted a fish near the bank.

I was about to catch it when a wild-looking creature I've never seen before slipped into the water. Then, quick as a blink, it snatched the fish away."

"What did it look like?" said Bracken.

"Let me see . . ." said Hazel, hiding a smile. "Silvery scales, fins, a tail . . ."

"Not the fish!" said Bracken. "The animal."

"Oh," said Hazel. "It had smooth dark brown fur. A white throat. A pale brown tummy. It was a good swimmer too! It took the fish in its mouth and sat on the bank to eat it – just where you're standing now."

Bracken looked down. Sure enough, he saw the remains of a fish tail.

"Now," said Hazel, "please leave me to catch another fish!"

"Good luck," said Bracken, and he set off again along the path.

Violet Vole and Hazel Heron had been helpful, but Bracken wanted to know more about the creature they'd seen. He wanted to see it for himself. Then he could tell his family all about it. He tried to imagine what animal had a long body, smooth dark brown fur, short legs and a thick tail that could swim and catch fish, but he couldn't think of one.

The five-toed prints went on and on. At last, Bracken came to a bend in the river. Daisy Duck was out with her ducklings. She saw Bracken and swam over to greet him.

"Quack, quack, quack!" said Daisy. "Where are you going all on your own?"

"Hello," said Bracken. He pointed to the path. "I'm following paw prints. Have you seen a strange animal about, Daisy?"

"Funny you should mention it," said Daisy. "I did. First, I heard a sort of whistling noise. Then I saw it with my own eyes. A wild-looking animal. It gave me the fright of my life!"

Bracken pricked his ears. "What happened?" he said.

"Well," said Daisy. "I was swimming with my ducklings down by River Island. . ."

"River Island!" said Bracken. "My friends Tansy and Teasel took me there once. Bramble, Berry, Fern and Wisher came too."

"Oh yes, it was a day I'll never forget!" said Daisy. "You and your marr helped to rescue my ducklings. If it hadn't been for you rabbits, they would have been swallowed by a horrid old pike!"

Bracken remembered the big fierce fish who lived near the island. He shivered. "It was very scary," he said.

"Anyway," said Daisy. "About this strange animal. It slipped into the river with hardly a ripple and dived underwater. Then it popped up right behind me!"

"What was it?" said Bracken.

"I've no idea," said Daisy. "But I didn't want it near my ducklings. It had a hungry look in its eye."

"Oh," said Bracken. He wondered if the strange animal ate rabbits too.

I can run fast, he thought. But what if the creature runs faster? Bracken was worried. Maybe he was being silly. Maybe this wasn't such a good plan after all. He remembered what his marr always said: 'Silly rabbits have careless habits!' But he was determined to be brave, so he asked Daisy anyway: "How far is River Island from here?"

"Around the bend and a few hops more," said Daisy. "Take care, Bracken. That wild animal is dangerous. It was swimming around the island when I last saw it. Quack, quack, quack!"

Return to River Island

3

Bracken watched Daisy go. The sun was high in the sky. He knew it must be about midday, which meant he'd been away from his burrow all morning. Bracken suddenly felt homesick, and very, very alone.

"Marr and Parr will be worried about me," he said. "The others will wonder where I am. And the wild animal might be very, very fierce! Maybe I should go home after all…"

He looked nervously about. He'd
been so busy following the paw prints
he'd quite forgotten to look out for
his enemies.

"I've been lucky so far," he said.
"Burdock the buzzard or a fox could
attack at any time. And Daisy Duck said
the strange animal looked dangerous.
But if I go home now, I'll be in trouble
for nothing, but if I find the mysterious
animal, I'll have something really
interesting to tell everyone. And I can
prove I was right about the whistling
noise. I'll show Bramble
I can be brave too!"

The thought of doing something to impress Bramble was enough for Bracken not to give up.

"I'll go to River Island!" he said.

After rounding the bend in the river and taking another twenty hops, Bracken found himself on a bank opposite River Island. It was a small island in the middle of the River Ripple with a waterfall at one end and a row of five stepping stones across the water, near the middle. Bracken shivered at the thought of crossing to the island on those slippery stones, each one a good leap apart.

It had been scary enough doing it with the others. He wasn't sure he was brave enough to do it on his own. But he really wanted to see the strange animal and prove to everyone he was right. And if that meant crossing the river . . . he would go!

Bracken remembered how their friends, Tansy and Teasel, the Greyback twins, had taken him and the others to see their secret place. Bracken looked towards the far end of the island for the old tree with a hollow trunk, and realised it wasn't there.

Then he saw that the tree had fallen into the river. It had made a sort of bridge from the bank to the island. Between the fallen tree and a thick bed of reeds the river flowed slowly and a shallow pool had formed.

Through the branches, Bracken could just make out the hollow, which had once been his friends' secret place. The opening lay on the top of the trunk.

Bracken was nervous. At any minute he might have to face the wild and dangerous creature. He looked around, hoping to see Tansy and Teasel, or his Elderparr and Eldermarr, Eyebright and Willow Silvercoat. There was no one about.

"Tansy and Teasel might be hiding in their secret place," he said to himself. "Maybe they know about the strange animal. I'll go and have a look. If they're not, I'll go to Burrow Bank and visit Elderparr Eyebright and Eldermarr Willow. It will be a surprise! I might see the twins there too. The Greybacks live next-burrow."

Bracken ran along the path to the
fallen tree. He was so excited at the
thought of seeing his friends again he'd
almost forgotten about the paw prints.

When he did remember and looked
down, Bracken saw that the first tracks
had now been joined by another set of
prints. A matching set, freshly made, and
coming from the opposite direction . . .

Bracken froze, ears pricked for any sound. Silence. Daisy Duck had told him she'd seen the stranger swimming around the island. Bracken tried to spot anything that moved, but only the flowing water caught his eye.

Bracken wondered if the wild beast was hiding, lying in wait and ready to attack. He wanted to run to his elders where he would be safe. But Burrow Bank lay on the far side of the tree.

"The secret place is nearer," he said. "If I see trouble, I'll hide in the hollow."

Bracken felt proud. He had worked out a plan all by himself, with no help from his bossy brother! Bramble usually took charge in scary situations.

He hopped along the tree trunk and stopped at the mouth of the hollow.

Then he peered into the darkness.
What he saw next made him gasp.

Four bright, round eyes stared up at
him. He could tell they didn't belong to
Tansy or Teasel!

He heard the snap of a dry twig.
Bracken spun around. To his horror,
Bracken found himself a whisker away
from the open jaws of a creature whose
lips were curled back from its teeth,
above a throat of snowy-white fur. It
looked very fierce!

Bracken jumped with fright, lost his balance and tumbled over backwards. He clawed at the tree bark and tried to save himself from falling in the river. Just in time, he grabbed a branch and held on tight, his hind legs dangling above the water. The animal looked at Bracken, hanging helplessly below.

"Oh, no!" he cried. "Please don't eat me! I should have stayed at home. I'll never see Marr and Parr or Bramble and Berry and Fern and Wisher ever again."

Double Trouble

4

Bracken kicked out wildly with his legs
and clung to the branch.
For a second he considered
letting go. Maybe he could
hide in the reeds until it
was safe to come out. Then
he remembered that
Hazel Heron had said
the animal was a
good swimmer.

It's no good, he thought miserably. Either way, this is the end. I don't like getting wet. I'll hang on and wait for it to eat me. . ."

Bracken didn't have to wait long. Powerful jaws gripped him by the scruff of his neck and pulled him on to the tree trunk. Bracken closed his eyes. He hoped being eaten wouldn't hurt too much.

What happened next took him by surprise.

"Now, young rabbit," said the animal. "What were you up to, sniffing around my holt? I have two young cubs in there."

Bracken blinked and blinked again. From the tone of her voice, he thought she sounded friendly. He hoped so anyway.

"Holt?" he said.

"My home," said the stranger. "When I first saw your gingery fur, I thought you were a fox!"

Bracken was amazed.

"A fox?" he said. "But that's silly."

"Yes, a silly mistake," she said.

Again the creature's lip curled from her teeth and, for a split-second, Bracken was afraid she might bite. But then he realised this was her way of smiling at him, even if it did look a bit scary.

"All I could see was your gingery coat," she went on. "It looked like fox fur. I thought you were after my babies!"

"I'm sorry," said Bracken. "I didn't mean any harm. I was looking for my friends, Tansy and Teasel. The hollow tree was their secret place."

"I see . . ." said the animal slowly. "That must have been before it blew down. There was a storm one night. Thunder and lightning and . . ."

She stopped as two small brown cubs appeared from the tree.

They huddled close to their mother, eyeing Bracken suspiciously.

"Who is he, Marr?" said one.

"Is he dangerous?" said the other.

"No," said their mother. "He's just a frightened little rabbit!"

Everyone introduced themselves.

"I'm Misty."

"I'm Silky."

"I'm Storm."

45

"And I'm Bracken Longears!"

Bracken looked at Misty, Storm and Silky. He still didn't know what they were.

"Please," he said politely. "What sort of animals are you?"

"We're OTTERS!" said Storm and Silky together.

"Where do you live, Bracken?" said Misty. "Do you have a family?"

"Yes," said Bracken. "I live with Marr and Parr and my brothers and sisters. Our burrow is in a meadow upriver."

"How did you find us?" said Misty.

"I followed your paw prints from the wooden bridge," said Bracken.

"Ah," said Misty. "Clever rabbit! I was hunting near there last night. I came home along the riverbank."

Bracken suddenly remembered the whistling noise in the night, and he asked Misty about it.

"That was me!" she said. "I was calling to my mate, Pad. He lives near there. We swam and played in the river."

"He's our parr," said Storm.

"He's bigger than Marr," said Silky.

Bracken thought it strange that Pad didn't live with his family. Bracken couldn't imagine not having his own parr around. It must be an otter thing, he decided.

The two otter cubs liked the look of Bracken.

"Come with us," said Storm.

"We'll show you around," said Silky.

"Okay," said Bracken. He knew
he should be getting back to his burrow,
but he didn't want to disappoint the cubs.

Besides, it would be fun getting to
know these strange new animals – it was
something Bramble had never done!
He couldn't wait to tell him all about them.
"I'll play for a while, then I must go home."

"Stay where I can see you," Misty said
to the cubs. "And keep your eyes open
for danger. I've heard a big old pike lives
around the island. So watch out!"

"You sound just like my marr!"
said Bracken.

"All mothers are the same," she said.
"We worry our whiskers off about our
children."

48

Bracken followed the cubs along the tree trunk and on to a muddy bank.

"Watch this!" said Storm, flopping on to his tummy. He slid down a slope and ended up – SPLASH! – in the river.

"Now me!" said Silky. She whizzed after her brother. "Your turn, Bracken," said Storm and Silky together.

Bracken loved sliding, but he didn't want to end up in the river. He chose a place where he could land at the water's edge. "Coming!" he said. **"Wheeeeee!"** He slithered down the slippery slope and landed with a bump at the bottom.

He was covered in wet mud from his ears to the tip of his tail.

"That was great!" he said.

At that moment, two grey rabbits
appeared at the top of the bank.
After Bracken had wiped the mud
from his eyes, he spotted them.
Both rabbits were exactly the same –
except one had straight ears and the
other's were floppy. It was his friends,
Tansy and Teasel.

"Tansy! Teasel!" shouted Bracken.

The twins stared back.

"Who's that?" said Tansy.

"A rabbit," said Teasel.

"Obviously," said Tansy, rolling her eyes. "Look. It's waving to us. How does it know our names?"

"Hi!" said Bracken. "It's me. Bracken Longears!"

"Bracken!" cried the twins. They raced down the bank to meet him.

"We didn't recognise you," said Tansy.

"Under all that mud," said Teasel. "We didn't know you were coming today."

"Neither did I," said Bracken. He told them about following the paw prints. "Then I went to look for you in your secret place and found . . ."

"Us!" said Storm and Silky.

The otter cubs, who'd been swimming underwater, suddenly came to the surface.

Tansy and Teasel were very surprised.

"Meet Storm and Silky," said Bracken.

"Hi!" said the twins nervously. Tansy and Teasel remembered finding three 'monsters' living in their secret place. The biggest one had looked so fierce the twins hadn't dared go back.

Tansy looked at Bracken.

"You're brave," she said.

"Thanks," said Bracken. "But I was scared of the cubs' marr too at first. Her name is Misty. She saved me from falling in the river."

"Wow!" said the twins.

Silky tugged at Bracken's tail.

"Come and play," she said. "You promised."

"Yes, I did!" said Bracken.

"Can we join in?" said Teasel. He thought Storm and Silky looked a wild pair and full of fun.

"Sliding in the mud is our favourite game," said Tansy.

"Of course!" said Storm.

"What are we waiting for?" said Silky.

"Race you to the top of the bank," said
Bracken. "One, two, three – go!"

The five friends lined up along the
muddy slope, then they slid all the
way down.

"Help!"

"I'm going too fast!"

"Here I come!"

"Look at me!"

"I can't stop!"

They landed in a heap at the bottom. There was so much mud it was difficult to tell rabbit from otter.

Misty smiled. She was pleased her cubs had made nice new friends.

Whispers
and a
Whistle
5

Back at the Longears' burrow, Mellow and Barley were very worried about Bracken. He had been missing all morning. Barley paced up and down, tugging his ear.

"Where has he got to?" he said.

"Who saw him last?" said Mellow.

The young rabbits tried to think what they'd been doing earlier when Bracken had been with them.

"We were eating cowslips," said Berry.

"Bracken saw them first," said Wisher.

"We all ran after him," said Fern.

"Er, I pushed him out of the way," said Bramble guiltily. "I think he was upset about that."

Mellow gave him a look. "Hm!" she said.

Wisher thought of something else.

"Bracken heard a whistling noise last night," she said. "We were cross because he woke us up, remember? And we didn't believe him."

"Yes!" said Bramble. "Because it was probably just the wind." But he felt bad about Bracken too.

"Ooo!" said Fern. "Maybe Bracken was right. Maybe he heard a monster whistling! What if it's caught Bracken? Oh, poor Bracken! He'll be eaten and we'll never see him again, EVER!"

Berry rolled his eyes. They were used to Fern imagining the worst.

Mellow tried to calm her down.

"We don't know that, Fern," she said. Suddenly she noticed Wisher had a faraway look in her eyes. "What is it, Wisher?"

"My ears are tingling," said Wisher.

The others knew what that meant. Wisher had special powers and often knew things before they happened. Whenever her ears tingled, it was a sure sign her powers were at work.

"I can hear a voice," said Wisher. "It's whispering inside my head."

"What does it say?" said Barley.

Wisher told them.

Slugs and snails! Slugs and snails!
A pathway of paw prints, tracks and trails.
Where do they go to? Follow and see
A secret place in a fallen tree.

"Slugs and snails is his favourite saying," said Berry.

"Oh, no," said Fern. "What if Bracken is chasing the whistling monster?"

"To the fallen tree," said Bramble.

"I think I know the one!" said Mellow. "It must be where we found you, Barley, that day you were swimming with some strange yellow ducks."

Barley remembered only too well.

"Let's go!" he said. "Oh, buttercups! I hope we're in time."

The rabbits raced towards the old tree. They had often used it as a bridge to cross to the other side.

Bramble led the way. When they found Bracken, he wanted to be the first to tell him he was sorry for being mean – especially about the cowslips. He'd eaten far too many flowers and they'd given him a tummy ache. And he missed Bracken terribly.

Barley and Mellow, Berry, Fern and Wisher chased after Bramble, and very soon all six Longears rabbits arrived at the fallen tree.

They searched around the roots and
branches and along the trunk, shouting
at the tops of their voices:

 "Bracken! Bracken!"

"Where are you?"

"I can't see him
anywhere."  "Nor can I."

 "He's definitely
not here."

"We've looked
everywhere."

Everyone looked at Wisher.

"Are you sure this is the right place?" said Bramble.

"Maybe not . . ." said Wisher slowly. "The voice said something about following paw prints to a secret place. I haven't seen any tracks, have you?"

"No," said Bramble.

The others shook their heads.

"You said we'd find the secret place in a fallen tree," said Mellow. "This is the only fallen tree I know, and here we are."

"Maybe Wisher's message was wrong about the tree?" said Fern. "A secret place could be ANYWHERE. We'll never find Bracken. He's gone for EVER!"

"Let's think," said Barley. "We can't give up now. We must find him."

Just then, Sylvia Squirrel came along.

"Hello," said Sylvia. "Good to see you out enjoying the sunshine. A pity Bracken isn't with you. He was a bit upset. . ."

"WHAT?" said Barley.

"You saw him?" said Mellow.

"Where?" said Wisher.

"This morning, by the wooden bridge," said Sylvia. "We had a chat about the whistling noise. I heard it too, but I've no idea what it was."

Everyone looked surprised.

"Bracken was right, after all,"
said Bramble.

"We should have believed him,"
said Berry.

"What happened next?" said Barley.

"I went to bury some acorns," said
Sylvia. "I left Bracken sitting by the
bridge. Oh, dear! I hope he's all right. I've
seen some strange animals about lately.
I shouldn't be surprised if that whistling
creature hasn't . . ."

"Yes, thank you, Sylvia," said Mellow.
"You've been a great help. Come on,
everybody. Bracken may still be by
the bridge!"

Barley, Mellow, Bramble, Berry, Fern
and Wisher ran as fast as they could to
the wooden bridge.

They searched above and below it,
but Bracken was nowhere to be seen.
Then Wisher gave a shout and pointed
to the path.

"Look, tracks!"

Barley examined them closely. There
were two sets of tracks – one set larger
than the other. "I know the paw prints of
a fox, a badger and a squirrel," he said.
"The larger ones are none of
those, but the other set belongs to a
small . . . rabbit!"

"Bracken?" said Mellow hopefully.

"Very likely," said Barley.

"Let's see where they go!" said Wisher.

The six rabbits hurried along the path, until they saw Violet Vole. She was sunning herself on the riverbank.

"Hello," said Violet.

"Sorry, Violet," said Barley. "Can't stop. We're looking for Bracken."

"Well, you're going the right way," said Violet. "I spoke to him this morning."

Barley stopped suddenly and the others piled into him.

"Parr!" said Bramble, Berry, Fern and Wisher, untangling their arms and legs.

"Was Bracken all right?" asked Mellow.

"I think so," said Violet. "He said he was on the trail of the whistling beast. I saw it with my own eyes last night. A wild-looking creature with the longest body you ever saw!"

"Oh," said Mellow. "What was Bracken thinking?"

"I'd watch out if I were you," said Violet.

"Thank you," said Barley. "We will."

Wisher took the lead and they continued following the paw prints.

It wasn't long before they met Hazel
Heron. She had just caught a fish.

"Hello, Hazel!" said Wisher. "Did
Bracken come this way?"

"Yes," said Hazel. "This morning. We talked about an animal he was tracking. He snatched a fish from me."

"Who? Bracken?" said Berry.

"No," said Hazel. "The wild beast! It was as slippery as an eel. It had sharp teeth too. It crunched up every bone."

"Ooo!" said Fern. She imagined how it would feel to be held in its jaws. "Poor Bracken will be eaten!"

"Not if we find him first," said Mellow firmly.

After thanking Hazel and saying goodbye, the rabbits rushed away.

Wisher's ears were tingling again.
The whispering voice was going round
and round inside her head:

Slugs and snails! Slugs and snails!
A pathway of paw prints, tracks and trails.
Where do they go to? Follow and see
A secret place in a fallen tree.

"I don't understand," Wisher said to
Fern, who was hopping beside her.
"We went to the fallen tree. Bracken
wasn't there."

"What about the secret place?"
said Fern. "That clue doesn't help
much either."

72

Just then, they saw Daisy Duck. She was on the bank, eating grass with her ducklings. She greeted them excitedly.

"Bracken's on the trail of a dangerous animal," quacked Daisy.
"It nearly ate my ducklings! I tried to warn him but I think he's gone to River Island to find it anyway."

"River Island!" cried the four young rabbits.

"Oh!" said Mellow. "This gets worse and worse."

"Oh, buttercups!" said Barley.

"Listen!" said Wisher. "What was that noise?"

The rabbits pricked their ears. What they heard was a long, low whistle.

An Old Enemy

6

Bracken, Tansy and Teasel, Storm and
Silky were playing in a shallow part of
the river, under the watchful eye of Misty
Otter. Sunlight sparkled on the water as
they splashed each other, shouting and
laughing.

They were having so much fun that no one noticed the long dark shape, lying still as a stone, hidden among the reeds . . .

After a little while, Storm said: "I'm hungry! I'm going to catch a fish!"

"Wait for me," said Silky.

Bracken, Tansy and Teasel saw the cubs dive underwater, leaving only a few ripples on the surface. They waited for a minute to see where they'd gone, but there was no sign of them.

"Where are they?" said Bracken.

Tansy saw some bubbles in the middle of the river.

"Over there," she said.

"They'll have to come up for air soon," said Teasel.

A quick movement on the riverbank caught the three young rabbits' attention. Misty had jumped down from the tree trunk. She stood alert, her eyes fixed on the water, searching for her babies. Then a small, silky dark brown head appeared. It was Storm.

"I caught a fish, Marr!" he said, paddling back to the riverbank with his prize.

"Well done," said Misty. "Where's Silky?"

"I don't know," said Storm, through a mouthful of fish. "I thought she was following me."

Bracken saw Misty's worried expression. He was worried too now.

"I hope she's okay," he said.

At that very moment, Bracken spotted Silky by a thick clump of reeds. He could see her whiskery nose, moving between the stalks. In a flash he remembered what had happened the last time he was at River Island.

"That's where Daisy's duckling was attacked by the pike," he said.

"Oh no!" said Tansy.

"We should have warned her," said Teasel.

"Silky!" cried Bracken. "Come back!"

Misty was already in the river and swimming towards her cub. To Bracken's horror, he saw a long, dark shape dart from reeds – fast. Scarily fast! Then Silky went under.

"Silky!" cried Storm.

"Oh no!" said Bracken, Tansy and Teasel.

They stood on the bank and could do nothing but watch. The water was crystal clear. They saw everything . . .

Misty dived. The pike had caught Silky by the very tip of her tail and she couldn't get away. But before the pike could get a better hold, Misty struck. With a thrust of her powerful tail she shot forward and took the pike by the throat. The pike's jaws sprang wide and Silky swam free.

"Hooray!" cheered Storm.

"Phew!" said Bracken.

"Swim to us," said Tansy.

"This way," said Teasel.

They could see Silky was still in danger. The rabbits and Storm looked on as Misty fought to keep hold of the monstrous fish. Their bodies rolled around, twisting and turning together as they struck upwards through the water, until they reached the surface.

Then, with the pike gripped firmly in her mouth, Misty swam to the water's edge.

"Slugs and snails!" said Bracken, staring at the pike's gaping jaws. "Look at those teeth!"

"Wow!" said Tansy.

"Not too near," said Teasel. "He might bite."

Storm and Silky, now happily back together again, crept forward to take a closer look. They sniffed.

"Mmm! Fish!" they said together.

For a few seconds, the pike beat its tail on the water – Slap-slap! Splish! Splish! Misty held the fish down until the flapping had stopped. At last, the big old pike lay lifeless at her feet.

Bracken stared at the fish, shocked at what he'd just seen. He was in awe of Misty. She was a fierce animal, brave and strong enough to fight a fish as big and mean as the old pike. He took a step nearer and said: "Is he dead?"

"Really, really dead?" said Tansy and Teasel.

"Yes," said Misty. "He put up a good fight and we must respect him for that. It was his nature to catch small prey like little otters."

She turned to Storm and Silky.

"Take care!" she said. "The old pike is no more, but there are other dangers."

Just then, they all heard a long, low whistle. Misty sat up. "I know that whistle," she said.

Storm and Silky did too. They looked and saw a dog-otter swimming towards them.

"Parr!" they shouted.

Misty greeted him happily. "You're just in time for a feast, Pad!" she said.

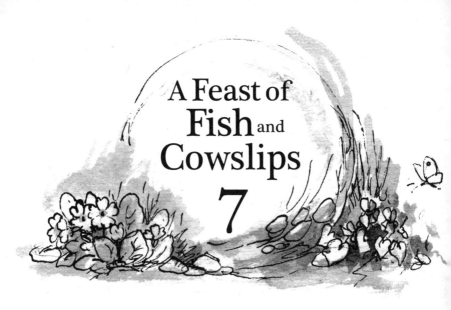

A Feast of Fish and Cowslips

7

"Bracken!"

The shout took Bracken by surprise. He turned to see Marr and Parr, Bramble, Berry, Fern and Wisher running towards him.

"There you are!" said Mellow crossly. "What were you thinking, running off on your own?"

"Silly rabbit!" said Barley. "We heard you were chasing a dangerous animal!"

"I'm glad you're okay," said Bramble. "I really, really missed you."

"We thought we'd never see you again!" said Fern.

"We were worried," said Berry.

"Very," said Wisher.

Then Mellow and Barley hugged Bracken so tight he could hardly breathe.

"How did you know where to find me?" he said at last.

"We followed a few clues," said Mellow.

"Wisher's ears," said Bramble.

"Sylvia Squirrel," said Berry.

"Violet Vole," said Fern.

"Hazel Heron and Daisy Duck!" said Wisher.

Barley was eyeing the otters suspiciously. He thought they looked like a wild bunch and wondered what sort of animals they were. Bracken introduced everyone.

"This is Misty and Pad, Storm and Silky," he said. "They're otters!"

"Hi!" said the Longears rabbits together.

"You must be Bracken's marr," said Misty to Mellow. "I knew you'd be wondering where Bracken was. He's been playing with my cubs."

"Oh, has he?" said Barley, looking hard at Bracken. "While you've been having fun, we've been worrying our whiskers off!"

"Sorry, Parr. Sorry, Marr," said Bracken. "But I wanted to find out who was making the whistling noise."

"It was us," said Pad. "It's the way we otters call to each other. Listen!" Misty and Pad gave each other a long, low whistle.

"You were right, after all," said Bramble to Bracken. "I should have believed you."

"Please, don't be too cross with him," said Misty to Barley. "He helped save my cub. Bracken has sharp eyes! He was the first to spot the pike."

"Ooo!" said Fern. "You were lucky it didn't eat you!"

"Scary!" said Berry.

"Well done, Bracken," said Bramble.

"My message didn't say anything about a pike," said Wisher. "Only paw prints and a secret place."

"I wasn't in danger from the pike," said Bracken. "I was a bit worried when I first met Misty though! But now we all have some new friends!"

Storm and Silky ran round and round. They were happy too.

Everyone was talking at once. Tansy and Teasel were excited to see the other young rabbits again.

It had been a while since they'd been together. There was such a commotion that lots of rabbits came out from their burrows to see what the fuss was about. First to arrive were Lop and Lilly Greyback, Tansy and Teasel's parents.

"Mellow!" said Lilly, greeting her old friend.

"Barley!" said Lop. "Good to see you again."

Then came Mellow's parents,
Eyebright and Willow Silvercoat. The
elders were so surprised to see everyone,
they had to sit down.

"This calls for a celebration!" said
Elderparr Eyebright. "I have a treat in
store for such a special occasion."

"What is it?" said Bracken.

"Ah!" said Elderparr Eyebright with a
twinkle in his eye. "Wait and see . . ."

He went away to collect something.

"We shall have a fine feast too," said Misty. "The old pike was the biggest one I've ever seen! There's plenty to share."

Pad, Storm and Silky clapped their paws.

"We can't wait!" they said.

The young rabbits wrinkled their noses.

"Yuck!" they said.

Mellow frowned. "Don't be rude," she said.

"Er, thanks," said Barley. "It's very kind of you, Misty. But we'll eat grass."

Then Elderparr Eyebright returned, his arms full of bright yellow flowers.

"Grass?" he said. "Oh, I think we can do better than that. I've brought some . . ."

"COWSLIPS!" said Bracken.

"Wriggly worms!" said Bramble.

"Creeping caterpillars!" said Berry.

"Bugs and beetles!" said Fern.

"Buzzy bees!" said Wisher.

Eldermarr Willow laughed. "Yes," she said. "Burrow Bank is full of cowslips at this time of year."

News spread quickly along the riverbank about the party. It wasn't long before Sylvia Squirrel, Violet Vole, Hazel Heron, Daisy Duck and her ducklings all arrived to join the fun.

There was enough fish and cowslips for everyone, and they ate until they were full.

Bramble came and sat beside Bracken.

"I'm sorry I was mean to you," he said. "You were brave to go off like that. I feel bad about everything that happened."

Bracken felt warm and fuzzy inside. He admired Bramble for being strong and taking charge when there was trouble. Bracken hated falling out with him. He was glad they were friends again.

"That's okay," said Bracken. "I didn't like being on my own. I missed everyone. It's much more fun when we do things together."

Later, as the sun was slipping behind the trees, everyone heard another whistle. It wasn't the long, low whistle of Misty and Pad calling to one another. This was a sound the rabbits knew well.

Bracken looked across the river towards two straight tracks that ran along the valley. Sure enough, he saw smoke and heard the rumble of something heavy as it thundered down the rails.

"The Red Dragon!" said Bracken.

"Going home," said Barley.

"It's time we were going too," said Mellow.

Barley and Mellow, Bramble, Bracken, Berry, Fern and Wisher said goodbye to everyone and went happily home to their burrow.